Chinchillas

Juliana Bartl

Everything About
Purchase, Care,
and Nutrition

Contents

36 Fit and Healthy

Appendix

The Typical Chinchilla

With their large eyes, their cuddly soft fur, and their bushy tails, chinchillas look irresistible. However, a word of caution: These cute rodents are somewhat eccentric and place rather particular demands on their owner.

Lovable Individualists

In earlier times, chinchillas were known particularly for their fur, which is unique in nature. In the meantime, however, these highly intelligent animals have conquered the hearts of more and more pet lovers. It is simply a lot of fun to experience and observe the highly active and curious chinchillas during their gymnastics and while they are on their discovery excursions; how they cleverly hold on to treats with their front paws, while nibbling on them. Because chinchillas are very sociable animals, it will not be long until you will be able to observe the entire chinchilla family during their games and other playful activities.

Pets with Special Demands

Chinchillas are, however, not quite the cute, cuddly animal that one is led to believe at first sight. They do not enjoy being handled by people. Sitting on a lap or an arm and being intensively petted is not a chinchilla's first choice. Only after the animals have become thoroughly tame do they enjoy being cautiously scratched under the chin, behind the ears, or on the belly, but—please—only after a chinchilla has approached the human on its own terms.

Therefore, chinchillas are not suitable as cuddly toys for children. Moreover, these largely nocturnal animals will only become active in the evening. During the day, they want to remain undisturbed in their sleeping quarters. Yet, for working people, who already have some experience keeping pets, chinchillas can be the perfect housemates. Prior to actually acquiring a chinchilla, you should educate yourself about the needs and requirements of these animals, and closely examine whether you are indeed able to provide sufficiently for these animals to guarantee them a happy and long life (see page 11).

A Brief Chinchilla History

It is helpful to have some knowledge about the origin and habitat of chinchillas: Knowing where and how they live in their natural environment offers appropriate conclusions about their demands and requirements as pets.

Chinchillas are native to the Andean Mountain region of South America. In the past, they ranged from Peru and Bolivia southward to Chile and Argentina, but are now found only in Chile and Bolivia. The name *chinchilla* comes from the Spanish conquistadores, but its meaning is uncertain. Chinchillas belong to the rodent family; their nearest relatives are guinea pigs, degus, viscacha, capybara, and also the South African porcupines. There are two chinchilla species in South America: the long-tailed and the short-tailed. Those animals kept as pets are long-tailed, distinguished from short-tailed chinchillas by a more delicate body and larger ears. Nowadays, there are many different color varieties (see pages 12/13).

Barren Homeland

In their native South American homeland, chinchillas live in colonies that number anywhere from 14 to 100 individuals. These colonies are made up of family groups of two to six animals each. They live in largely barren mountain regions at elevations of up to 13,123 feet (4,000 m), where there is little vegetation. Short-tailed chinchillas can even be found at elevations up to 16,404 feet (5,000 m). There, chinchillas hide principally in rocky crevices or in caves during the day. These regions are characterized by large contrasts in climate:

› The habitat of chinchillas is very dry. The average precipitation is only about 7.9 inches (200 mm) per year. Rain falls principally during their cold winter months from May to August, generally in severe showers during the midday hours. The remainder of the year is dry.

› The temperatures in that part of the Andes mountains vary substantially. During the summer

The much larger viscachas are close relatives of chinchillas. They occupy similar habitats in the Andes mountains.

months, the mercury can reach more than 104°F (40°C), but at night the temperatures can drop down to about 32°F (0°C).

Very Well Adapted

Chinchillas have adapted very well to these extreme conditions:

> Their thick fur, up to 1.2 inches (3 cm) thick and made up of the finest of hairs, provides excellent protection against the cold. However, chinchilla fur is extremely sensitive to wetness—the individual hairs tend to stick together and the fur no longer can fulfill its function as insulation against the cold. Therefore, chinchillas sleep through the rain showers securely covered in rocky crevices and caves.

> Even the high-noon temperatures cannot harm these rodents in their habitat: As crepuscular and nocturnal animals, active at dawn and dusk, they sleep during the noon hours in shaded locations among crevices and in caves. In these locations, temperatures never exceed 68°–72°F (20°–22°C) even on the hottest summer days.

From the environmental conditions of the chinchillas' habitat, one can see what conditions are needed for those kept as pets. Although these chinchillas can also tolerate very cold conditions, they have considerable problems handling temperatures in excess of 68°F (20°C). The optimal temperature range for chinchillas in captivity should be a relatively even 64°–68°F (18°–20°C).

The Long Way to Europe

South American Indians had kept chinchillas as pets and to provide fur for clothing. For the Spanish conquistadores, the trade with the silky, soft furs of chinchillas quickly became a profitable business: The animals were easy to collect during the day

In the wild, chinchillas spend the day in rocky crevices and caves. There, they are protected from rain as well as extreme heat.

when they were sleeping in rocky crevices. However, the animals were being hunted well in excess of sustainability, so that as early as the end of the 19th century, chinchillas nearly became extinct. Although hunting chinchillas is now forbidden, these animals continue to be endangered due to habitat destruction by agriculture and through mining. Finally, in 1983, a chinchilla reservation was established in northern Chile. In this area, there is sufficient room for the animals, and scientists are able to investigate the complete natural history of the chinchillas. However, population levels of wild chinchillas are recovering only gradually.

Chinchillas were first taken to North America as breeding stock for fur production. From there they went to Europe in the middle of the 20th century, where they are still being bred for their furs. In North America, chinchillas were discovered as pets during the 1970s and 1980s.

Anatomy and Senses

Tail

A conspicuous feature of chinchillas is the bushy tail; it is nearly as long as the body. For chinchillas, it is a piece of sporting equipment as well as a mood barometer; it serves as a counterweight for the body when jumping, as well as a rudder. Various tail positions, together with raising the tail hairs, convey the mood of the animals.

Fur

The most conspicuous feature of chinchillas is their silky, soft fur. A single hair root gives rise to up to 60 individual hairs. This way, perfect heat insulation is being created. Since chinchillas have neither sweat nor sebaceous glands, the fur cannot cope with wetness.

Paws

The front paws of chinchillas resemble small hands. The animals use them to handle their food and then manipulate the food skillfully into their mouths. The soles of the hind paws are rubberlike; their balls provide support while climbing and cushion jumps. Instead of claws, the paws have nails that are similar to our fingernails.

Ears

Chinchillas can hear the slightest noise due to their large, movable ears. In addition, these heat-sensitive animals regulate their body temperature with the aid of large *pinna* (external ears): because the ears have extensive blood vessels, they give off excess heat.

Eyes

At nightfall, chinchillas wake up. At that time, these animals—much like cats—can see very well at dusk as well as in total darkness with their large eyes. On the other hand, during the day they squint with pupils restricted to a narrow slit. Because the eyes are located laterally on the head, chinchillas can see very well what is happening all around them as well as overhead—the best life insurance against enemies, such as small predators or birds of prey.

Nose

The nose of chinchillas is not only there to sniff, but it is also the location of long, highly sensitive, tactile hairs. With the aid of these, chinchillas can not only find their way around in darkness, but they are also able to measure distances. That makes them agile climbers and jumpers.

Brief Chinchilla Profile

Chinchillas are clearly distinguishable from their nearest relatives based on certain characteristics:

› Chinchillas measure 8.3–12 inches (21–30 cm) from the tip of the nose to the base of the tail, and the bushy tail adds another 6.3–7.9 inches (16–20 cm).

› A fully grown chinchilla weighs on average 12.35–24.7 ounces (350–700 g). The male, called a buck, is often smaller than the female, however size and weight can vary. There are delicate animals with "model" measurements, which never reach a weight in excess of 17.64 ounces (500 g). On the other hand, large breeding animals can weigh up to 2.2 pounds (1 kg).

1 In males, approximately .4 inch (1 cm) above the anal opening, the round penis can be seen. The testicles are not always visible because they can be retracted into the abdominal cavity.

2 Females have a vaginal cone that extends downward terminating into a point. This can be seen clearly just above the anal opening, which is located slightly below.

› As rodents, chinchillas reach a surprisingly old age. With proper care, they can easily live for 10 to 15 years, some even for 22 years.

› Chinchillas can reach sexual maturity as early as 3 to 5 months; they are fully mature at 12 to 18 months.

› Males and females are difficult to distinguish. It takes some experience to identify the sexes with certainty (see illustrations 1 and 2), an important factor when males and females are to be separated during estrus, when the female is in heat.

› The incisors of chinchillas are difficult to overlook; their enamel is bright orange. In chinchillas, all teeth grow continuously throughout their lives, and they are constantly being worn down by gnawing and chewing.

› The most conspicuous characteristic of chinchillas is the silky, soft fur, which forms a thick heat insulation. Up to 60 individual hairs grow from a single root. These hairs point in all directions, and so the chinchilla's fur does not show any streaking. Wild chinchillas are light to dark gray; now there are many different color varieties among captive-bred animals (see pages 12/13).

Keen Senses

Chinchillas are perfectly equipped with appropriate senses for a life in darkness.

› As with many other nocturnal animals, their large eyes are conspicuous; with them, chinchillas can orient themselves perfectly in darkness.

› The tactile hairs on the snout also facilitate movements in the dark.

› The large, funnel-shaped ears enable chinchillas to hear the softest noise. Moreover, they also serve—as on other desert animals—to give off excess heat. Because chinchillas cannot sweat, they have to regulate their body temperature this way.

› Chinchillas have an excellent sense of taste and smell. They will sniff at everything. After that, a test bite decides whether they like a certain food or not. Even that which is inedible will be gnawed on.

Clever Mobility Artists

Chinchillas have relatively short front paws and strong hind legs. Therefore, they move in a hopping manner—much like rabbits. The front paws merely serve as support and as skillful manipulating organs. Only when chinchillas move more rapidly do they show how athletic they are: From a standing position, they can jump up to 3.28 feet (1 m) high. The tail serves as a rudder and gives the animal appropriate balance when jumping.

What About Other Pets?

If you decide to get chinchillas, you should—if possible—not have any other pets. As much as chinchillas enjoy the company of their own kind, they are a world apart from dogs and cats.
› Guinea pigs, rabbits, and other rodents are active during the day and will therefore disturb chinchillas when they are sleeping. Moreover, chinchillas will get sick when they nibble from the food of other animals.
› Chinchillas are prey for dogs and cats, even if these have been raised to be very gentle and are well trained. The presence of such predators means permanent stress for chinchillas.
› Birds make a lot of noise during the day and will disturb chinchillas. Moreover, large ornamental birds tend to remind chinchillas of birds of prey.
› Even an aquarium does not belong near the chinchillas; the high humidity will cause the individual hairs of their fur to stick together, thus causing a loss of insulation.

Will Chinchillas **Suit Me?**

These questions will help you decide whether chinchillas are the right pets for you.

MANY YEARS OF RESPONSIBILITY Chinchillas reach an age of approximately 15 years. Are you willing to look after these animals for that long? Would you be able to organize proper care and maintenance when you are on vacation?

SUFFICIENT ROOM Do you have room for their cage, approximately 59.1–79 inches (150–200 cm) high and 40 inches (100 cm) wide?

FREE RUN Will you be able to provide a secure area for these animals to run freely (see page 26)?

TIME Will you be able to spend at least two hours per day to look after your chinchillas?

SPECIAL CONSIDERATION During the day, chinchillas require a quiet environment so that they can sleep undisturbed. Are you willing to do without music and television?

DIRT AND GNAW MARKS Will you be able to live with sand and animal bedding around the cage and gnaw marks on the furniture?

COSTS Apart from the purchase costs, can you handle $60.00 per month to feed and care for them, plus $25–$125 per year for veterinary expenses?

Chinchilla Portraits

Whether blond, brown, or black, apart from chinchillas that look like their wild ancestors, there are now chinchillas in many different color mutations—and all have their charm.

WHITE MOSAIC Gray and white alternate with each other. Base of tail, ears, and the fur around the eyes is gray. Feet and nose are pink and the eyes are dark.

DARK TAN Brown chinchillas are chocolate brown from head to tail. Even the abdomen is brown, but sometimes slightly lighter colored than the fur along the back. The eyes are dark red; the nose and hands are light pink.

EBONY Completely black from head, abdomen, and back to the tail; only the gray-colored ears provide a contrast to the dark fur.

STANDARD This is the coloration of wild chinchillas. The tips of hairs are mottled light-to-dark gray; the roots of hairs are dark gray and the abdomen is white.

VIOLET Attractive color mix: head, back, flanks, and tail are gray with a hint of lilac. The abdomen is shiny white and the eyes are black.

BLACK VELVET Back and head are black with a velvety sheen. Attractive contrast: gray flanks and ears, white abdomen, and gray-black tail.

BEIGE These chinchillas have a fur that is mottled in beige color tones, the abdomen is white, and the eyes are red. Characteristic: With increasing age, there are brown spots on the pink ears.

BEIGE-BLOND Among beige color varieties, there are also various graduations from brown to almost completely white. In light-colored blond chinchillas, the ears, feet, and nose are pink.

Interpreting Chinchilla Language

Chinchillas have a large sound repertoire: For these social animals that live in groups, sounds are the most important form of communication, apart from smells and body language. Chinchillas "talk" to one another in order to show that they belong together, to warn one another of dangers, or to protest when they are feeling under pressure from other members of the group. It is not only fun to recognize the meanings of these various sounds, but it also tells you what is happening at a particular moment in your chinchilla family. Moreover, a short "chinchilla language course" is also important so that you can interpret alarm signals correctly and react promptly when there is stress among your pets.

The Most Important Chinchilla Sounds

The following different sounds are ways chinchillas communicate among one another.

"I am here!"—The location call. The sound is the most frequent "word" in the chinchilla language. It consists of many consecutive low-volume, high-frequency tones. This sound sequence is most commonly used when chinchillas are on the move within their territory. This way the animals indicate where they are and so maintain contact with the other members of the group. Especially the hierarchy leader of the group gives off this location sound, as well as those animals that are particularly curious and have a strongly developed explorer drive. However, in most instances, there is no specifically recognizable reaction among the other chinchillas in the group.

"Come here, I have discovered something"— The attractant call. This particular call is also a contact sound. It is reminiscent of a soft gurgling and consists of up to ten individual sounds. Chinchillas give off this attractant call when they have discovered a new object in the territory or a particularly tasty treat. The other chinchillas react by either sitting up and pointing their ears toward the caller or sniffing the air and then running over to the animal that has called. Alternatively, they will run toward the calling animal immediately after the call has been made; then they will sniff at one another's noses and examine what the caller has discovered. If several members of the chinchilla group are on a discovery tour, individual animals will give off an attractant call alternately—often in combination with a location call.

"Stop it! Don't do that!"—The clicking sound. This short sound is reminiscent of tongue clicking or coughing. It is given off by chinchillas, for instance, if they have been bitten too hard during the mutual grooming session, or if they have been disturbed while feeding or sleeping. To do that, the chinchilla shakes its head sharply. In most

Chinchilla **Baby Talk**

CONTACT SOUND Newborn chinchillas give off a loud chirping sound, which is their way of establishing contact with their mother. The babies react with this sound to the sniffing of their mother. It indicates that the young are healthy and active.

SUCTION SOUNDS These sounds are reminiscent of a cross between whimpering and chirping. Chinchilla babies will give off this sound when they are suckling and feeling very comfortable.

instances, the other animal reacts immediately and will stop. If not, the bitten chinchilla will give off another clicking sound. The longer the disturbance lasts, the more clicking sounds are given off consecutively by the affected animal. Similarly, this sound is also made when people pick up chinchillas. In that case, you should respect that your chinchilla does not like it and you should leave the animal alone. Maternal chinchillas also give off clicking sounds when the young are biting too aggressively while suckling.

"Leave me alone"—The defensive sound. This is a more inconspicuous sound, which is short and reminiscent of a croaking. It signals that another chinchilla or a human should keep its distance or should go away. An example: A chinchilla male enjoys a dust bath and another male approaches. In response, the male in the dust bath will give off the defensive sound. The approaching male will initially stop, and then after hearing a second defensive sound, it will retreat.

"Caution! Danger approaching"—The alarm call. This is often the first call a chinchilla owner hears, because it is particularly loud and shrill. It can be heard also throughout the day. Since the animals never go into a very deep sleep, they perceive the slightest disturbances. In nature, this ability protects chinchillas against approaching dangers.

The alarm call consists of several, rhythmically linked individual sounds whereby the first sound is the loudest. Chinchillas are very sensitive animals. They get frightened by loud and unfamiliar sounds, as well as by abrupt movements among group members.

Similarly, they can get frightened when a human enters the room. However, this call serves primarily as an alarm call within the group: If one of the animals gives off an alarm call, all other chinchillas immediately interrupt their activity and leave the cage floor, to flee as quickly as possible to the upper sitting platforms or into the sleeping dens. After a few minutes, they emerge from their hiding

No welcome here: "Leave me alone" is being indicated by the chinchilla inside the tube. The other female will have to look for other company.

places again, alert and with erect ears. If there is no further alarm call, they will continue their interrupted activities.

"I am angry" or "I am terribly scared"—The panic call. Only in an instance of extreme aggression and panic will chinchillas emit this scream. The animals are very afraid, angry, and under extreme stress. However, it can also be heard when a female is giving birth and another female in the group is pregnant. In that case, the animals are afraid of the competition within a territory that is too small. Similarly, when two cages containing males that are hostile toward each other are placed too close together or there is no sight barrier, the animals will often emit this call. When this happens, the chinchillas involved will get up on their hind legs and extend their upper bodies forward, raising the snout and slightly opening the mouth so that the teeth are visible. The ears and the tactile hairs are folded back, but the hairs on the tail are conspicuously erect.

This call is an alarm signal that you must take very seriously. When you are keeping your chinchillas under optimum conditions, you will rarely ever hear this call. However, if you hear it frequently you should make efforts to find out what

Courtesy is essential: Chinchillas greet each other by pressing nose against nose when their paths cross. The animals recognize each other based on smell, which suggests to them: This chinchilla belongs to my group.

scares your chinchillas, and then proceed to eliminate the causes as quickly as possible.

Somewhat Complicated: Teeth Grinding

There are several different variants of teeth-grinding noises among chinchillas. All have rather different meanings.

"Leave me in peace; I am scared." This variant of teeth grinding is a threat. For that, the chinchillas click their teeth rapidly so that it sounds almost like hissing. The threatening chinchilla sits up on its hind legs; the upper body is bent slightly forward, but totally extended so that it appears as large as possible. The front legs are hanging down. This type of teeth grinding is used principally among same-sex chinchillas. For instance, animals will emit this sound along the territorial border toward animals of the neighboring group. If chinchillas use teeth grinding toward humans, they feel trapped—for instance, when the human attempts to catch them.

"I am in pain." Teeth grinding that consists of individual slow-grinding movements signals that an animal is in pain. Often a chinchilla is then in a resting position or it may be feeding. When you hear this type of teeth grinding, you should observe the animal closely and consult a veterinarian as soon as possible in order to find the cause of the pain and eliminate it.

"I am very well." However, teeth grinding can also be a sign of thorough enjoyment. For instance, when chinchillas cuddle up to each other or they are taking a dust bath, they slowly and quite audibly grind their teeth together. For the uninitiated chinchilla keeper this sound is difficult to distinguish from the exclamation of pain. Observe your animals closely. If you are not sure what the grinding means, you should consult a veterinarian.

Is My Chinchilla **All Right?**

TIPS FROM
THE CHINCHILLA
EXPERT
Dr. Juliana Bartl

Be receptive to the sounds of your chinchillas, and learn the various sounds given off by the animals as quickly as possible.

LOCATION CALL AND ATTRACTANT CALL
When a chinchilla is giving off either of these sounds (see page 14) everything is okay: The animal is healthy, happy, and active.

CLICKING AND DEFENSIVE SOUNDS These sounds are used to resolve minor disagreements among the animals. Within a stable chinchilla family, these sounds are likely to occur occasionally. However, if this happens too often you should attempt to resolve the cause and—if need be—eliminate it.

ALARM CALL When you hear the alarm call, danger is approaching. What could be the reason your chinchillas are afraid? Is the location of the cage optimal? Could the animals be suffering due to excessive noise? Eliminate the reason for such an alarm call.

PANIC SCREAM This scream means severe aggression. Is there strong tension within the group? In such a case, you may have to alter the group's composition.

At a Glance: Posture and Body Language

Chinchillas not only "talk" among one another, but they also communicate by means of a diverse body language. Watch your chinchillas closely! The better you understand your animals, the faster the trust will grow between you and these sensitive little rodents. Very important: You must also accept a "no" from your chinchillas. If you do that, there is nothing to obstruct the pathway to a close relationship between you and your chinchillas.

1 Please Do Not Disturb!

Chinchillas are sitting on all paws or have one front paw slightly raised, making a fist, which means: "I am sleeping and I do not want to be disturbed!" Ears are close to the body, the eyelids are partially closed. Under no circumstances should you wake them. That would stress the animals and eventually make them ill.

2 Everything Is Okay!

Awake chinchillas like to sit on their hind legs with their "hands" free. In that posture, they survey their surroundings or feed, looking particularly cute holding food in their front paws. Even when resting, chinchillas prefer to sit in that position. The tail is relaxed or slightly coiled, resting on the ground.

3 Bless You!

A chinchilla poked its nose too deeply into a pile of hay and will skillfully wipe off with its front paws whatever is making it sneeze. This gesture is also an appeasement, or it indicates embarrassment.

4 Hello, There You Are!

Once your chinchillas have gained sufficient trust in you, they charge out of their sleeping hut and over toward the wire as soon as you approach the cage. Often the animals will hang on to the wire with their front paws and sniff with their noses held up in the air. This is their way of establishing contact with the human owner. Could there be a tasty treat for us? Chinchillas greet one another by rubbing their noses together or by sniffing the other's anal region. As a demonstration of mutual affection, they also tend to nibble on one another's fur.

5 This Is My Territory!

Chinchillas are self-assured territory owners: They will mark their possession with a raised tail and a little bit of urine. To animals from another group, this odor signals: *Halt—this is not your place!* If a chinchilla of the same sex, but from another group, approaches the territorial border, chinchillas can get extremely upset. In that case, the ears are laid flat against the head; the animals display their teeth and hiss or scream. In addition, the long hairs on the tail will be erected into little tufts. If that does not work, they will use the ultimate weapon: They rise up on their hind legs and spray a stream of urine in the direction of the enemy.

6 Attention Everybody!

When chinchilla males sit back on their hind legs, erecting the entire body and ears, and bunching up the tail hairs in patches, they are directing the tactile hairs and the ears toward the source of a particular noise. Your chinchillas apparently heard something exciting. Check whether everything is okay or whether danger is approaching.

Finally at Home

Before your new pets can move in with you, there are still a few things that need to be considered and prepared for. Have you found a reliable chinchilla breeder already? How many chinchillas can you accommodate? Has the cage been furnished properly?

Off to a Good Start

By deciding to get chinchillas, you have opted for some very fascinating animals; however, they will also place certain demands on you. Depending upon the breed, chinchillas can cost anywhere from $75–$250. In addition to that, a large cage, whether it is prefabricated or you have made it yourself, as well as some basic furnishings will add another $300–$500. Then there are costs for food and sand, as well as veterinary expenses (see page 11).

Privacy Is Desired

Is not exactly easy to find the correct location for the chinchilla cage. The climate during the North American summer months is often too hot for these animals. Dampness can be a problem, too, because the fur of chinchillas cannot handle wetness. Therefore, balcony or garden visits— even for short periods—should never be allowed.

In your home, chinchillas require a location that is protected against heat, direct sunshine, and drafty conditions.

> The ideal situation would be if you could provide a room just for chinchillas, and even install an air-conditioning unit.
> Such a room also has other advantages: Chinchillas are sensitive creatures, and they should not be disturbed during the day when they are asleep. Also, you will have peace at night, when the chinchillas are particularly active. It is amazing how much noise these little rodents can make.
> Alternatively, you can set up the cage in a cool living room, where it should be located along one wall. This way, you cannot walk around the cage completely, which would make the animals nervous.
> It is essential that you place the cage on a table or on some other support frame, and NOT directly on the floor: Chinchillas will get frightened when you bend over the cage. To these little rodents, anything that comes from above means that a potential danger is approaching, such as birds of prey.

One Chinchilla Never Thrives Alone

Under no circumstances should chinchillas ever be kept as solitary specimens. They are family animals with a comprehensive social behavior. Chinchillas like to cuddle up closely to one another when they are sleeping; they like to go out on discovery excursions together and then "chat" extensively with one another. Even while feeding, the chinchilla family sits together. Therefore, you should get yourself several chinchillas; animals kept alone feel lonely and eventually will become ill.

The Perfect Group

Whether it is a mini-group of only two chinchillas or—better yet—a group of four to six animals, the rules for the combination of the sexes are always the same. It is not yet known exactly how chinchillas live in the wild. Presumably, a group consists of several females—grandmothers, mothers, and daughters, headed by a single male. Juvenile males are driven out of the group as soon as they have become sexually mature, but female juveniles often stay in the group.

Male and female For a group of chinchillas kept together in a home, it is ideal to have a single male together with three to five females. For instance, this can be a mated pair and its offspring. Pure sibling constellations are also possible. So that there will be no undesired offspring, you will need to do estrus checks on a regular basis, and then keep the male separate from the females for a few days (see page 56). For that, you should have separate accommodations ready, possibly by setting up the main cage with provisions for inserting a partition or a false floor. This way, the animals are separated

from one another but sight-odor contact between them is being maintained so that the social unity remains ensured.

Castrating chinchilla males is not advisable, since this affects their behavior, and the group no longer accepts them. This can inflict substantial suffering on the males so that they may ultimately die. Moreover, chinchillas are very skilled with their front paws and will often tear out or gnaw the stitches from the operation. Serious inflammations are often the consequence of this.

Same-sex groups If kits—baby chinchillas—are not desired and when estrus control and separating animals appear to be too cumbersome, it is better to decide on a group of four to six animals of the same sex. This works best when the animals have grown up together. Sisters, but also mother and daughters get along quite well. Similarly, several males raised together usually also get along with one another, since there will be no rivalry for a female.

Only Acceptance Counts

Fundamentally, assembling chinchillas that have not grown up together into a group is rather difficult. It is particularly problematic to add a single animal to an already existing group. In such a case, it is irrelevant whether you are adding a buck to a mixed group or a new female to an all-female group. Moreover, females will not necessarily accept every buck. Very experienced chinchilla keepers are sometimes able to integrate a new animal into an existing chinchilla group, however, there are no recipes for success—even among chinchillas, acceptance cannot be forced. Either the animals like one another at first sight, or they simply cannot stand one another. There are often fights resulting in severe injuries on both sides. Moreover, social stress and fighting usually create psychological damage; the defeated animals stop feeding, become ill and ultimately die.

If you are forced to put different chinchillas together into a group, you should first test whether the hoped-for friendship has indeed a chance. To do that you hold—with the aid of another person—both animals firmly so that they can sniff each other. If they hiss at each other and become aggressive, there is no point in pursuing this matter further. In that case, the only choice you have is to keep the animals separately. For such an event, you should always keep a spare cage ready. If you would like to assemble a group of animals from different litters, it is advisable to consult a professional breeder (see page 24). He knows best the character of his animals and can assemble a group for you. The animals thus selected will then jointly move into their new territory at your home.

The Right Age

Sometimes young chinchillas are removed from their mothers at seven to eight weeks. That is too early. Although chinchillas will start feeding on their own at four to six weeks and are no longer dependent on mother's milk, they still need to learn many social behavior details from their parents, so that they can handle life in a chinchilla group without problems. If you are buying young chinchillas, they should be three to five months old.

Never alone: Whether feeding, sleeping, or during the daily discovery tour—only in a group is life fun for chinchillas.

Cohabitation Options

The following composition of chinchilla groups has proven to be effective:

CLASSIC FAMILY Parental pair together with daughters—even from different litters. Important: maintain estrus control, prevent father-daughter mating.

SIBLINGS Two to three siblings—males and females—from the same litter. Important: estrus control, prevent mating.

FEMALE COMMUNITY Group of four to six related females.

MALE COMMUNITY Un-castrated, same-age bucks that have grown up together.

The Time Has Come: Purchase and Transport

Take your time when buying your chinchilla. After all, you are about to enter a long-term partnership.

› Keeping chinchillas is expensive. Usually they are offered as live pairs. You must never buy individually kept chinchillas. Such animals can hardly ever be integrated into an existing chinchilla group. On the other hand, old animals kept in a group will readily adapt to a new owner.

› The largest selection (together with professional advice) is usually available from professional chinchilla breeders. Hobby breeders usually offer their animals via the Internet.

› You can also ask your veterinarian and make inquiries with an animal shelter about chinchillas that are in need of a new home. Whether it is a pet store or a professional or hobby breeder, you must always keep the following points in mind:

First-class journey home: the chinchillas feel secure in an animal carrier, and will get over the transport [almost] stress free.

› The be-all and end-all of a good purchase is detailed professional advice.

› Responsible breeders produce at least 30 animals a year so closely related animals are not crossbred with each other. Moreover, experienced breeders make sure that the parents are not too young when they are being mated. Both of these factors can cause the health of the offspring to suffer, and reduce longevity.

› Experienced breeders know that some color varieties must not be crossbred because the offspring of such crosses would be unhealthy and have a limited life expectancy.

The First Contact

Arrange for an appointment with a breeder or pet store in the early evening hours for your first visit. That is when chinchillas are awake, and you can assess whether they are healthy and active. Their behavior and character can be judged as well, rather than when they are tired.

The following will assist in your evaluation:

› The eyes must be clear and the fur around the eyes must not be matted. Moreover, there must not be any discharge from the nose.

› The abdomen of chinchillas must be free of greasy, brownish yellowish patches.

› The fur must be dense and fluffy, and there must not be any bare patches.

› If an animal is wet around the chin, it means that there are dental problems.

› It is also important that the anal area is clean. Traces of fecal material are a sign of diarrhea.

› Normal teeth are a yellowish orange color.

Safely Home

Since every transport means stress for chinchillas, you should look for a breeder in your vicinity:

› This avoids long transit times. Because they are heat sensitive, bring the animals home on a day no hotter than 70°F (21°C), unless you have a car with air-conditioning.

› Buy an animal carrier designed for cats from a pet store. It will come in handy when taking them to a veterinarian. A cardboard box is not suitable.

› It is advisable that the breeder puts the animals into the carrier; he knows best how to handle the animals correctly (see page 35).

› Take a little bit of food along from the previous owner to prevent any digestive problems due to an immediate change in diet.

› Chinchillas feel more secure during the declining light of dusk. Therefore, place a cover over the carrier. This also protects the animals against drafts.

› If a longer transport is unavoidable, offer your animals a little bit of hay and some apple pieces. Water should be provided during transport rest stops (the standard chinchilla watering containers usually spill during the trip).

The First Few Hours at Home

At home, the new cage must of course be fully ready so that the chinchillas can quickly move in.

› Place the open carrier inside the cage or against the door opening, and then move back. Give the chinchillas time to climb out of the box. The curious animals will quickly conquer their new home.

› During the first few weeks, the animals remain in their cage to explore their new territory.

› Do not pick up the animals until they are fully tame. That, too, requires a bit of training (see page 35).

Chinchillas on **the Internet**

TIPS FROM
THE CHINCHILLA
EXPERT
Dr. Juliana Bartl

Many chinchilla keepers offer animals via the Internet. The following criteria will help you to find hobby breeders you can trust.

SPECIALIST BREEDER KNOWLEDGE Inquire about the parents' and grandparents' health, the age of the mother (she must be at least two years old), and what litter this is (out of a total number of litters produced). He shouldn't be breeding with too many different color varieties.

PROXIMITY Choose a breeder who lives no farther than three hours of driving time from you. Long transport times mean substantial stress for chinchillas. Chinchillas must never be "dispatched" by couriers or similar transport means. That could be fatal for the animals.

PERSONAL PICKUP Inspect the animals on-site to assess their character and health, and the conditions under which they are kept.

INTERNET FORUMS These are ideal for the exchange of information with other chinchilla keepers, but save questions of behavior, nutrition, and health for your veterinarian.

A Feel-Good Home for Chinchillas

Although chinchillas are allowed to enjoy the evening free run, they will spend the largest amount of their time in a cage. Therefore, it is important that the cage be as large as possible and be optimally furnished to meet all the requirements of these animals. It goes without saying, that the minimal requirements for keeping these pets need to be met (see page 28). Having said that, you may want to substantially increase the space available for your chinchillas beyond the basic requirements.

> For a group of four to five chinchillas, the cage should be 5–6 feet (150–200 cm) high and long as well as 3–3½ feet (100 cm) wide. A sufficient height is important so that you can install at least three to four levels of additional platforms, or sitting boards. Only with that much space are chinchillas able to roam about to their hearts' desires and jump from one platform to another.

> Large cages made of wood or metal are available from pet stores. On the Internet, you will be able to find suppliers of various models of rodent cages in different sizes. Some suppliers will also offer custom-made units as per your requirements.

> Rabbit cages are not suitable because they are too low and too small. Similarly, birdcages cannot be recommended because they usually do not withstand the takeoff power of chinchillas when jumping.

> The cage should be fitted with sitting platforms and running boards at several levels, which are all interconnected through steps or climbing branches (see page 29). Make sure that these boards do not extend only along the cage walls, but that the center of the cage is also utilized, by installing bridges, connecting branches, or tubes of some sort. Partition boards, with a hole in the middle for a chinchilla to fit through, are also useful.

> The basic structural unit of the cage should be made of untreated lumber. The sidewalls and a door should consist of metal mesh or wire mesh. They must not be stained or painted. Even often-recommended galvanized cages are not suitable.

A perfect fit. Everything a chinchilla's heart desires can be provided by a cage you have built yourself.

Chinchillas will chew on anything and can easily get sick because of poisoning from paints or galvanized surfaces. The floor of the cage should consist of lumber or smooth plywood. A bottom tray made of aluminum needs to be covered by a layer of litter.

› Products made of plastic are totally taboo. The animals will chew on this material and get sick.

› If a ferret cage is purchased, any plastic shelves and ramps provided with the cage should be replaced with thick wooden shelves and ramps.

Chinchilla Cages

An excellent alternative to commercially available cages are cages built at home. With some skill and handyman work, you can build your own chinchilla cage to fit perfectly in the space available, and to provide optimum room for your group of chinchillas.

The same fundamentals outlined above for commercially available cages also apply for the do-it-yourself models. The cage and furnishings must be absolutely safe and gnaw proof.

› The wire mesh of the sidewalls must be sufficiently rigid, so that it can withstand the jumps by the chinchillas, as well as supporting them when they are climbing up on it.

› Make sure that the individual mesh openings are not too large, so that chinchillas or their eventual offspring cannot escape from the cage.

› The interior furnishings, such as sitting boards, climbing branches, and ladders, must be secured with screws or similar devices so that they cannot move, causing the animals to sustain injuries while using them.

Things to remember when **building a chinchilla home**

CAGE STRUCTURE	THINGS TO REMEMBER	THIS IS IMPORTANT, BECAUSE . . .
FRAMEWORK	Use untreated lumber. Firmly screwed together; use strong angle and diagonal bracing.	Chinchillas chew on wood and can poison themselves when ingesting paint components. Chinchillas are powerful jumpers.
WIRE/MESH	Non-coated, at least 0.6 inch (1.45 mm) diameter wire. Open wire ends must not protrude into the cage.	Chinchillas can poison themselves by gnawing on rubber coating; sharp wire ends can cause injuries to the animals.
SIGHT BARRIER	Two to three cage walls and part of the roof must be covered.	Chinchillas require sight protection from above and if facing other cages.
RETREAT FACILITIES	Caves and crevices must be sufficiently large: provide two entrances.	Chinchillas must be able to avoid each other in case of physical arguments.
BOARDS AND ELEVATED PLATFORMS	Not too steep and not too far apart, interconnected with ladders and ramps.	Chinchillas tend to jump onto barely reachable platforms, and could injure themselves if they fall.

Cage Furnishings: All You Need for a Chinchilla Villa

Chinchillas like to run around, jump, and climb inside their cage in their continuous search for new adventure. However, at the same time, they also need opportunities to withdraw to rest. Therefore, do not scrimp on outfitting the cage, because this is what makes the cage an ideal chinchilla home.

At All Levels: Sitting Boards

The larger the cage, the more sitting boards should be available for the animals. You should attach these boards horizontally along the cage walls. This provides different levels for the chinchillas to utilize the entire cage space available. The distances between the boards should be 12–20 inches (30–50 cm). This enables the chinchillas to jump easily from one board to the next. The material used should be untreated wood. If the cage walls are made of wood, these boards can be secured with angle irons screwed into the wall. In wire cages, the boards can be suspended by means of special hooks.

Comfortably Bedded: The Sleeping Hut

So that your chinchillas can sleep soundly in total security, they require separate sleeping huts in their cage. These huts should be approximately 12 inches (30 cm) wide, 8 inches (20 cm) high, and 20 inches (50 cm) wide, and should be attached at various levels in the upper third of the cage. Although several chinchillas may sleep in one hut, there should be one sleeping den per animal available, just in case the family peace is temporarily shattered.

› Wooden huts, such as those used for guinea pigs and rabbits, are also suitable. These should be attached in the upper section of the cage, screwed onto a sitting board.

› Bird nest boxes are also a good choice, provided the entrance has a diameter of 4–6 inches (10–15 cm).

› Some chinchillas like sleeping huts that have two access holes. Since several of these animals like to sleep together, it is sometimes easier for individuals to leave when it is getting too crowded inside. A tube made of cork bark with a diameter of approximately 6 inches (15 cm) is suitable for that purpose.

Climbing Branches, Stairways, Bridges

No chinchilla cage without branches! The animals use them for climbing; together with stairways

---

For a **contented chinchilla**

HOUSING The larger the cage, the better. Recommended size is 5–6 feet (1.5–1.8m) high and long by 3–3½ feet (.9–1 m) wide. It must have a solid floor, protection from direct sunlight, one sitting board per animal, a dust bath of at least 100 square inches (250 cm²), and one sleeping hut per animal, which can (if need be) accommodate all animals in the cage.

NOISE Chinchillas are very sensitive to noise. Therefore, living rooms and children's rooms are not suitable locations for the cage. Make sure that television sets and stereo equipment in your home are sufficiently far away from the chinchillas.

HEAT Although chinchillas periodically like a little bit of sunshine, they must always be able to retreat into the shade. The temperature in the cage must never exceed 68°F (20°C).

This is a comfortable place to rest: Several animals can cuddle up tightly in a sleeping tube made of cork.

Can I chew on this sleeping hut? Nothing is safe against chinchilla teeth. Therefore, the entire cage furnishings must be made out of untreated timber.

and bridges, they become a perfect fitness course. Sufficient opportunities for movement and activities not only keep boredom away, but also provide for the animals' fitness. However, since chinchillas use branches not only for climbing, but also to chew on, you must make sure that they are made of safe wood, such as that of apple or pear trees that have not been sprayed with pesticides (see pages 40/41).

Toilet and Bedding

Chinchillas distribute their feces throughout the cage, however they usually urinate in particular corners. There you can offer them a toilet in the form of a box or a large bowl filled with hay. In order to mark their territory, chinchillas will also urinate in the proximity of their feeding place or at a main intersection of commonly traveled paths. Quite unsuitable as toilets are the plastic toilet boxes for rabbits available from pet stores. These are quickly chewed to pieces by chinchillas.

Bedding Chinchillas do not need any bedding or litter in their cage. It is easier for the animals to get around on a smooth floor without any bedding, because this gives them better traction for jumping. If you do not like an empty floor, you can cover it with special small animal bedding made of hemp fibers.

Only the floor area in the toilet corners or where the toilet box is needs to be covered (for hygienic reasons) with a 2-inch (5 cm) thick layer of litter. The cage is then easier to keep clean. Best suited for that purpose is special pet litter. Unsuitable are so-called straw pellets (also called natural straw and natural wood litter). Similarly, an empty metal or wire mesh floor is not good for the animals. These materials damage the delicate skin on the soles of the animals' feet. Pure sawdust creates a lot of dust. Similarly, cat litter, bark mulch, potting soil, or exotic animal litter made of wood have no place in a chinchilla's cage, because it is possible that the animals will actually feed on the material and become sick.

Absolutely Essential:
The Dust/Sand Bath

The daily dust/sand bath is a creature comfort for body and soul for all chinchillas. Rolling around in the sand is good not only for the fur so that it can fulfill its function as a warming hair cushion, but it is also a means of reducing stress and providing relaxation for the animals. Therefore, a dust bath must be accessible to chinchillas. Large bowls or dishes not made of plastic can serve as "bath tubs." They must be heavy enough so that they cannot be moved about by the animals. Ideally suited are chinchilla bath boxes that are fitted with a hook and can be suspended from cage walls. Even highly energetic rolling around by chinchillas inside the box cannot tip it over.

The sand bath must be sufficiently large so that several animals can bathe at the same time. If you have more than three chinchillas in a cage, it is advisable to place two or more sand baths inside the cage.

The correct sand You should use only quartz-free, special chinchilla dust or sand for filling the sand bath. Common sand—available from building suppliers—and bird sand are totally unsuitable. Both of these are too rough and will damage the sensitive chinchilla skin (see Information).

Feeding Bowls

All feeding containers must be able to withstand the chinchilla temperament—otherwise they will be pushed around the cage by the playful animals. Sometimes, chinchillas also like to sit on the rim of a food container.

› Therefore, only heavy earthenware or ceramic bowls that have a wide, inward-pointing rim are suitable. Moreover, they need to be secured so that they do not slide or tip over in the cage. Food dispensers for pellets are generally attached to the outside of the cage.

› Hay should be offered in a special hayrack, which cannot be used as a toilet or the hay becomes soiled and wet. It is advisable to use wide, closed racks, made of wood or metal. Such a hayrack should be installed in the cage in such a way that it terminates just below a sitting board so that the chinchillas cannot climb into it and soil the hay.

Caution Hayracks made of wire mesh or a hay ball suspended by a chain can become a trap for chinchillas, if their feet are caught in the rack's interspaces or in the suspension chain.

My tip Garden centers sell terra-cotta or ceramic bowls. These are ideally suited as hay troughs, where the chinchillas can pull the hay out through the openings. Important: All these containers must not be lacquered or painted.

Drinking containers You can use regular rodent drinking bottles as water dispensers. These bottles are attached to the outside of the cage and must be replenished daily. Water bowls are not recommended—the water will get dirty very quickly.

Use Only the **Best Quality Dust/Sand**

TEST Not everything that is offered as chinchilla dust or sand is of suitable quality. You can use a simple test to check whether a product meets the requirements of these animals: let the sand run through your fingers. Quality sand does not scratch, but it is soft. Afterward, the skin should feel very dry. Such sand is suitable to remove any traces of wetness and grease from the fur of chinchillas, without damaging the skin of the animal.

FUR CARE The daily dust/sand bath is vital for chinchillas. The dust/sand removes wetness and grease from the fine-haired fur. This is the only way the multitude of tiny hairs can form a proper heat-insulating cushion. For chinchillas in their natural habitat, proper care of their fur is a survival necessity: Only a fluffy fur protects sufficiently against wetness and cold. The same applies to pet chinchillas; they will only remain healthy if they can have a dust/sand bath.

WELLNESS The soul also takes a bath! Enthusiastic rolling around in the sand helps chinchillas to reduce stress. Small arguments with some of the other members of the group or the excitement of the most recent free run adventures can simply be forgotten when in the sand bath. Therefore, do not be surprised when these little fellows will roll around extensively in their sand bath several times a day.

WELL CARED FOR After the bath, all the sand is shaken out of the fur. With freshly groomed fur, the animal climbs out of the dust/sand bath, ready for new adventures.

Chinchilla Rhythm: When Night Becomes Day

Chinchillas are crepuscular and nocturnal animals, active at dawn and dusk, and as their owner, one should respect that. Sometimes they adapt to our daily schedule and will welcome you in the morning, in order to get a treat. However, chinchillas that are regularly woken up during the day will suffer stress and gradually become ill—even when there are initially no symptoms.

Brief Chinchilla Diary

Are you at home much during the day? If not, you will welcome the biorhythm of chinchillas. It is usually evening by the time these animals are fully awake.
Sleeping time While we humans are at work, chinchillas are generally in peaceful slumber. During the day, they are asleep most of the time—preferably huddling on all fours, cuddled closely together in their sleeping hut.

Scientists have learned that the sleep of chinchillas consists of up to 140 phases, composed of discrete segments, each lasting 5 to 7 minutes, which alternates with deep sleep phases lasting 2 to 3 minutes. Caution: Even during these phases, the animals will readily wake up at the slightest noise. Sometimes, chinchillas will also sleep during the day unprotected in the cage. For that, they rest on sitting boards or on food bowls. There they keep

Well rested, the chinchilla emerges in the morning from its sleeping hut.

Gnawing is fun. Nothing gives chinchillas more pleasure than to chew branches and lots of other material into small pieces.

their head lowered and the ears are flat against the head. Even when the eyelids are only partially closed, you should not disturb the animals—they are, nevertheless, in sound, deep sleep. During the afternoon hours, chinchillas sometimes spend extended deep sleep phases lying on one side. If at that time a ray of sunshine enters the cage, they stretch their body in obvious enjoyment.

During the entire sleep period—approximately between 9 A.M. and 3 P.M.—chinchillas rarely feed. If they get up at all, it is only for a quick bite.

Time to get up In late afternoon or during the period of sunset, chinchillas become active again. Their "day" might start with a dust bath, in order to clean the fur that has become ruffled while asleep. Then it is time to groom. Chinchillas are very fastidious animals; not only do they clean themselves, but also the other members in the group. This makes grooming not only more effective, but it also strengthens social bonds.

Feeding time Slowly the chinchillas are getting hungry. Although they feed throughout the entire night until about 7 A.M. the main feeding is between 9 and 11 P.M. at night. In terms of table manners, this may leave something to be desired: Chinchillas are "culinary experts," they tend to rummage through their food bowl in search of their favorite foods. Anything that does not taste very well is forcefully tossed aside and scattered through the entire cage.

On discovery tours Once the first hunger pain has been stilled, the chinchillas embark on exploring their territory. Is there something new to be discovered somewhere? The animals run around in a playful manner, demolish branches at great speed, and chew on anything they can find.

Free run Once your chinchillas have become tame, that is the time for the daily free run. Usually the

Even that tastes good! Gnawing is not only an activity. The bark of branches contains important nutrients and vitamins.

animals can hardly wait to leave the cage and embark on their adventure tour. Social contacts must also be maintained: If animals cross each other's path, they rub their noses together and sniff each other's anal region, as well as chewing on each other's fur. In between, they have little rest periods on some elevated sitting platform, but their ears remain fully erect so that nothing is missed. On the other hand, could there be danger approaching?

When Night Becomes Day At the latest, the animals must be returned to the cage when they appear to get tired (see page 53). Of course, that is not yet the end of playing and roughhousing, enjoying the adventures of the free run, taking a sand bath, and tumbling around in the hay. Only when it is time for you to get up has the time come for chinchillas to go off to bed!

How to Tame Chinchillas

Tameness precedes trust—you have to give yourself a few months to conquer the new pet's shyness. Keep in mind that chinchillas are still wild animals. Do not force the issue; otherwise, any fresh bond with the animals will be destroyed for a long time. Never try to handle your chinchillas while they are not yet completely tame. Even after the animals are starting to trust you, leave the first step to them. Eventually your chinchillas will approach you and then quickly climb onto your shoulders.

Establishing Trust: Step-by-Step

The taming process for chinchillas proceeds over many steps. These can be subdivided into three phases. When you keep practicing these steps with your chinchillas, they will soon start to trust you. Depending on the character of individual animals, these phases vary in length of time. Especially young animals are often rather curious, so that they will quickly establish contact with you. Valid for all phases: Always approach the animals slowly, talking to them with a calm voice.

1st phase During this phase, the cage door always remains closed, so that the animals feel secure. Think of an identifying noise—for instance a soft tongue clicking. You must always make this noise when you enter the room with the chinchilla cage. The animals learn quickly that this clicking sound means "hello." The following steps should be practiced during the first week after the chinchillas have moved into your house. Repeat this sound often, while the animals are awake.

› Enter the room, clicking your tongue. At that stage, the chinchillas are still very shy. They will hide as soon as you come near.

› After a day or two, the chinchillas will still flee to their sleeping hut, but they will remain in front of it. The animals are watching you closely, sniffing the air, raising their ears, and listening to your voice. However, they are always ready to flee.

› Even during the following days, the chinchillas will flee to their sleeping huts as soon as you enter the room. However, they will watch you closely and react with eye contact or with movements of the tactile hairs when you are quietly talking to them.

2nd phase As soon as the animals no longer flee when you enter the room, the second phase begins. You still enter the room with the identifying sound. The cage door remains closed. However, you approach the cage closer and offer treats through the wire. Practice that for a month or so, several times a day. (So as not to promote diarrhea, try small chunks of hay blocks, or divide a slice of dried apple into several pieces, giving out the pieces one at a time throughout the day.)

› The chinchillas are still taking off when you approach the cage; however, they come to the cage wire. They sniff at the treat, but lack the courage and will quickly run away again.

› Finally the ice breaks: As soon as you enter the room, the chinchillas will come running to the wire and sniff in your direction. They sit up on their hind legs and hold on to the wire.

› At that point, the chinchillas will come directly to the wire and will take the treat from your hand and taste it with a quick bite. Then a slight residual fear takes over again. They run off without the treat and watch you from a distance.

1 Can I risk it? During the first few weeks, the chinchillas are still distrusting. First, they have to get used to your voice and your smell.

2 Curiosity wins: After a few days behind the safe wire, the chinchilla risks taking a treat from your hand cautiously.

3 Only good things come from this hand! After a few weeks, you can hold your hand through the open cage door: The chinchilla knows you and is no longer afraid.

4 Patience is being rewarded with trust. Eventually, the chinchilla risks a test bite from your finger, and soon the animal will climb cautiously onto your hand.

› Success! The chinchillas approach the wire and take treats from your hand. They will eat them inside their sleeping hut.

› Almost routine: The chinchillas come over, accept the treat, but remain at the wire while eating it.

3rd phase As soon as the animals are tame, the third phase begins. Keep entering the room with the identification sound, but now cautiously open the cage door. Practice the following steps several times daily for about three months.

› The chinchillas are coming to the cage door. What is the treat going to be today? Maybe they venture a test bite from your finger. Finally, the animals place their front paws onto your finger. They take the treat and eat it while sitting in front of you.

› Extend your arm further into the cage. Now one of the chinchillas will try to climb onto your hand or your arm. Finally, the animal climbs out of the cage and onto your body.

› At that stage, the chinchillas can be touched on their front paws and can be scratched on the chest and behind the ears. However, their back and tail remain off limits.

Picking Up Chinchillas Correctly

When chinchillas are so tame they will climb onto your arm, you should be able to pick them up.

› Let the chinchilla sniff your hand. Then gently slide one hand under its chest and reach with the other hand over the back of the animal. Pick it up and transfer it quickly onto your body, making sure it does not jump off and injure itself.

› Caution: When stressed, chinchillas can cast off patches of fur to protect themselves. If you grab your pet by the fur, the patch of fur will release from the chinchilla's skin so it can escape.

› Breeders hold chinchillas at the base of the tail with one hand and support the abdomen with the other. This requires practice. Never hold them by the end of the tail: that hurts and leads to injuries.

Fit and Healthy

A healthy diet and proper care will ensure a long life for chinchillas. Yet, these curious rodents require more: They must be able to discover new things continuously during their daily free run in search of adventures. That includes extensive climbing, running about, and jumping. When they can do that, there is nothing to prevent a chinchilla's happiness!

What Makes Chinchillas Completely Contented?

Every day you should set sufficient time aside for your chinchillas; to feed them and for routine maintenance, and to observe them during their free run and while they are playing. On one hand, it is a lot of fun, and on the other, it guarantees that you know exactly that everything is okay with your animals.

Room Service and Fitness Program

In their native habitat, chinchillas are used to a meager diet, and so the body of our chinchillas has become perfectly adapted to such paltry nutrition. With their powerful gnawing teeth they are even able to chew on woody plant branches. For that, the extremely long intestine, the caecum, as well as special intestinal bacteria, ensure that all the important nutrients are removed from this type of food. In the wild, chinchillas spend many hours each day searching for food. Anything they come across is manipulated with their front paws to the mouth and tested with the characteristic test bite: Is the morsel edible or not? This type of food search not only provides for diversity and activity, but also keeps these highly active rodents very fit.

On the other hand, our chinchillas no longer have to spend endless hours in search of food. They get their food essentially "delivered free of charge," fresh every day. So that boredom does not strike the chinchillas and the animals get enough exercise, it is essential that we provide them with an appropriate activity and fitness program. Keep building new things inside the cage, such as tubes to hide in, suspension bridges from and to a new climbing branch, etc. However, the high point of every day is the free run: Then the chinchillas can play around to their hearts delight with the other members of the group.

What Chinchillas Like to Eat

Make sure that the dietary plan for your chinchillas is healthy and diverse: Hay and pellets are a sound nutritional basis that should be supplemented by herbs and some fresh food (see page 40).

Hay—Aromatic and Healthy

The ideal basic food for chinchillas is high quality, fresh hay. This must always be available to the animal in abundance, even during the day. Hay is important for the nutrition of chinchillas for diverse reasons:

1 Fresh, quality hay contains up to 80 different plants: apart from various grasses, there are also flowers and herbs.

2 Not only is taste important—shape and size also play a role: Pellets should be elongated, so that the animals can easily hold them in their front paws.

> Hay includes a substantial component of raw fibers. This supports a healthy intestinal flora and provides for proper digestion. The long threads of hay stalks on their path through the digestive track take along any swallowed hairs, and so protect the animals against blockages by fur balls.
> Hay stalks are tough. This forces chinchillas to chew extensively, and so the incisor and molar teeth of these rodents are worn down in a natural manner.

Quality is essential The more diverse the plant food mixture is, the better is its quality! Moreover, quality hay provides the animals with many vitamins and minerals. Pet stores offer various hay products.

> Make sure that the hay is fresh and dry. Depending upon the type of plants, it should have a green to slightly yellow color and have an aromatic smell.
> Be aware of dusty, old or even musty-smelling, damp and fungus-covered hay. Such inferior quality hay must never be given to chinchillas, because fungus makes the animals sick.

Pellets—Excellent for Nibbling On

Pet shops have special chinchilla pellets for sale that are made from a mixture of grasses, Lucerne hay, and herbs. They are also fortified with minerals and vitamins. Make sure you check the composition details listed on the package. Quality products consist of raw fibers, raw protein, calcium, and phosphorus. The pellets must not be too thin, but should be sufficiently long so that the animals can easily hold them with their front paws.

Caution—this makes fat It is important to avoid at all cost mixtures containing oats, raisins, sunflower seeds, and pumpkin seeds. These ingredients lead to excessive weight gain in chinchillas and will harm their intestinal flora.

Herbs Keep Chinchillas Fit

The following varieties are healthy for chinchillas: milk thistle, coneflowers, rose blossom, nettle, dandelion, peppermint, and lemon balm. Ideally, you should offer your chinchillas a different variety or mixture every week—this provides variety in the food bowl.

However, many other herbs are not suitable for chinchillas: because such herbs are also used as herbal medicines, they often have a specific effect on the body. This is not always immediately noticeable in the animals, and sometimes does not manifest itself for months or even years.

Recipe In my experience, the following mixture has proven to be effective; however, do not modify the amounts of the different components—otherwise there can be an undesirable effect:

> 1 oz (6 tsp) [30 g] each: rose flower leaves, cone flowers [leaves, stems, and flowers], dandelion, and
> .71 oz (4 tsp) [20 g] each: rose hips [dried], nettle, peppermint, as well as
> .35 oz (2 tsp) [10 g] each: sage leaves, lemon balm leaves, cornflowers, yarrow, ginkgo leaves, chamomile leaves, raspberry leaves, and strawberries.

Basic **Feeding Rules**

TIPS FROM THE CHINCHILLA EXPERT
Dr. Juliana Bartl

FIXED FEEDING TIMES Chinchillas are creatures of habit. Therefore, you should feed them every day at the same time. The early evening hours have proven to be the most effective, when the animals are wide-awake and active. At that time, you feed pellets and fresh food. However, hay and herbs should be available throughout the entire day.

THE CORRECT AMOUNT Per day and animal, you should feed a handful of hay, 1 teaspoon of pellets, and 3 to 4 teaspoons of herbs. Fresh food is given only twice or three times a week—about 2 teaspoons per animal is sufficient (see page 40).

CONTROLS Check whether your chinchillas have actually eaten the food provided, by first removing any leftovers from the earlier feeding.

HYGIENE Remove any leftover foods daily, so that the animals do not feed on soiled or—worse—even spoiled food.

NO SUDDEN CHANGES Avoid sudden dietary changes—chinchillas invariably react with digestive disorders. New food items should be given initially only in small amounts.

Fresh Food Within Limits

Unlike guinea pigs, chinchillas do not require daily portions of fruit and vegetables. Two or three times a week of this type of food in small amounts is a welcome change. However, you should introduce your chinchillas slowly to fruit and vegetables in order to avoid digestive disorders. Because individual chinchillas have distinct food preferences, you have to try patiently to find out what the animals like and what they do not like.

> Many chinchillas like a piece of fresh apple (with the skin left on) or pear, but most other types of fruit are too wet or sticky.

> A fresh carrot, parsley, dandelion leaves that have not been sprayed with pesticides, and rose flower leaves, fit well into their diet plan.

> A real treat for chinchillas are the leaves and stems of a Jerusalem artichoke. That is always a hit with these animals, regardless of whether it is fresh or dried, and it also facilitates digestion.

My Tip This bulbous plant is readily cultivated in a garden or even on a balcony. It can be easily dried by suspending it under cover, for use during the winter.

> Kitchen herbs like parsley, nettle, dill, lemon balm, and thyme are not only tasty, but they also create activities for chinchillas: set up herb pots, which can then be placed in the cage or in the area used for free runs, so that the animals can essentially "serve" themselves.

> The hit among herbal snacks is the daylily, a mineral-rich plant with a high water content. Chinchillas like to hold the leaves with their front paws and then nibble on them.

Calcium tablets and others If chinchillas are given a variable diet, they will not need vitamin

Caution: Toxic – Even Small Amounts Can Make Chinchillas Sick!	
FRUIT	cherries, rhubarb, plums
VEGETABLES	eggplant, avocado, legumes, potatoes, garlic, all cabbage, kohlrabi, leek, corn (maize), Swiss chard, horseradish, radish, (red)beets (dried flakes from pet shops are tolerable), all types of lettuce, spinach, onions
WOOD	azalea, berberis, birch, box (tree), beech, oak, black alder, laburnum, elder, chestnut, cherry laurel, (common) privet, coniferous woods, especially yew (tree) and thuja, bursting heart (American strawberry bush), rhododendron
ORNAMENTAL PLANTS	aloe, cyclamen, amaryllis, anemones, azalea, weeping fig, calla, Christmas rose, Christ's thorn, chrysanthemum, dieffenbachia, ivy, ferns, fuchsia, geranium, hortensia, hyacinth, coral tree, oleander, orchids, philodendron, primrose, wax flower, Christmas star, and many others
HAY	Check hay before feeding: even quality hay can contain meadow saffron and sorrel. Both are toxic for chinchillas
OTHERS	Bread, cookies (biscuits), chips, chocolate

Tastes are variable: Chinchillas like to pick out their personal favorites from the food bowl.

Fresh food on a stick. There is nothing better than aromatic green herbs—especially when they can be held so easily.

supplements, salt stones, or calcium tablets, unless a veterinarian prescribes these.

Anything to Gnaw On: Branches and More

Branches and twigs are regular components of the chinchilla diet; however, they serve principally as their favorite activity, i.e., chewing and reducing stress. However, not all types of wood are suitable. Apple and pear tree, hazelnut, raspberry, and willow can be given without concern. Of course, leaves are left on the branches. However, the branches of certain other trees are toxic (see page 40).

Gnawing stones Chinchillas love to gnaw on blocks of pumice stone. However, only buy pumice stone chews made for small animals. The animals keep chewing on them until all edges have been gnawed off smoothly. At that point, you should break up the stones or saw new edges into the stones—that encourages the chinchillas to chew on

them again. Similarly, untreated pieces of wood also satisfy the gnawing instinct. However, quite unsuitable are so-called gnawing sticks, gnawing crackers, and hay bells; these items usually contain sugar or honey, substances which are not healthy for chinchillas.

Fresh Water Must Always Be Available

In the wild, chinchillas cover their water needs through the intake of vegetable matter. As pets, they must always have access to fresh water; one animal drinks approximately 0.7–1.4 ounces (20–40 ml) water a day. Water bottles for small pets have proven to be effective. In some regions, tap water is very hard (dissolved calcareous matter). That can lead to the formation of bladder and kidney stones in chinchillas. Therefore, it is advisable to filter tap water or—better yet—give your animals non-carbonated mineral water with low calcium content. Milk, tea, and other drinks are totally taboo for chinchillas; they cannot tolerate it.

An Occasional Treat Is Allowed

Even chinchillas can be bribed: A tasty treat will help to overcome their initial shyness and will help to train them. Later on, the odd tasty treat can indeed work miracles—when you are trying to coax your chinchillas onto a scale for checking their weight, or when the animals are supposed to return to their cage after their free run.

Yet, what tastes good is usually not very healthy. Therefore, offer treats to your chinchillas only individually, by hand, and never put several treats into the cage. Too many will not only make your animals sick, but you will also spoil their appetite for healthy hay.

What Is Allowed?

Even if you give only a few tasty treats, you should make sure that these are not too unhealthy; for instance, nuts should be eliminated right from the start, because they are too fattening.

> Dried fruits, especially pieces of apple, are excellent treats. The animals can easily handle these with their front paws, and they are sufficiently large to keep chinchillas busy briefly, so that there may be enough time to quickly weigh the animals or close the cage door.

> Raisins have high sugar content. They are allowed as "bribes" under exceptional circumstances and for particularly difficult cases only. A special treat for chinchillas are fruit bars from health food stores. However, because of the levels of sugar, flour, and nuts, only tiny pieces should be given to the animals.

> You can also spoil the animals occasionally with pea flakes, carob, nibble rings, and oatmeal cookies (all available from pet stores).

Delicious temptation: Certain treats even weaken the "toughest" chinchilla. This way you can easily coax the animal back in to the cage after its free run.

So Chinchillas Can Stay Healthy

Often chinchillas get sick because they have been fed an incorrect diet. Therefore, feed your animals only the correct food: that is the basis for chinchillas remaining healthy and fit for many years to come.

What to Do

 Hay is the basic nutritional component in the diet of chinchillas. It ensures an excellent intestinal flora, and because the stems must be chewed for a considerable period, the teeth remain short.

Chinchillas must chew a long time on hay cobs (see page 50). That provides activity and prevents dental problems. Similarly, pieces of different types of wood are also popular materials to chew on.

 Treats of dried apple pieces or rose hips are a delicious and healthy reward.

 The crowning glory in the food bowl is fresh herbal leaves. Your chinchillas like them; they promote good health, and provide diversity.

What Not to Do

Cereal products in dry food, as well as oatmeal, upset the digestion of chinchillas and make them ill.

Hard, dry bread softens in the mouth of chinchillas. It does not contribute to the important dental wear, but, instead, leads to digestive problems.

Not every herbal plant is suitable for chinchillas to chew on. Talk to an experienced veterinarian about it.

Commercially available chewing sticks and crackers often contain too much cereal and sugar. Therefore, they are unsuitable for chinchillas.

The Chinchilla Home: Always Neat and Clean

Chinchillas are very clean animals and they make sure that their fur is always clean. They particularly enjoy mutual grooming with other chinchillas of the group. All you have to do is establish the prerequisites for proper chinchilla care and the animals do the rest. For that, one most important item that must be available to the animals is a sufficiently large dust/sand bath (see page 30).

Hygiene Is Essential

Chinchillas need a well-maintained home in order to stay healthy and feel comfortable in their surroundings with you. The daily cage cleaning can easily be done in the morning, when the chinchillas are asleep. No doubt, the little rodents will have left behind their "marks" in the cage during their nocturnal fun and games. However, you can also clean and tidy up the cage at other times of the

Unable to chew it into smaller pieces? No problem for chinchillas: their teeth—tough as steel—can even handle pumice stone chews.

day. Yet, it is important to stick to a particular time of the day when performing these tasks. Once the animals know your routine, they will not stress out when they hear the unmistakable cleaning sounds.

What Needs to Be Done

Certain maintenance tasks need to be done daily, others once a week, or even once a month.

Daily maintenance During your morning inspection, you will immediately notice that the chinchillas love to scatter their food throughout the entire cage.

> Even when hay, prepared foods, herbs, or fresh food still look good the next morning, all leftover food should be removed daily. It can make chinchillas sick when they eat wilted or even decomposing food. So you do not have to throw away too much, give smaller daily feedings, closely adjusted to the animals' requirements.

> Drinking water must be changed daily. You should brush the water bottle in hot water without any cleaning agents, using a specific bottlebrush, and paying close attention to the actual drinking spout (bottle opening).

> The food bowls must also be cleaned daily, using hot water without any cleaning agents.

> The sand bath must be cleaned of fecal balls, straw, etc., daily. This is best done by straining the sand through a fine mesh kitchen strainer.

> Change the litter in the toilet corners—that saves time because then the entire cage needs to be cleaned out thoroughly only once a week.

> Clean all sitting boards and climbing branches with the aid of a small broom, to get rid of fecal balls, hay, and uneaten food.

Important Do not forget to check all cage equipment. Are the climbing branches, sitting boards, or sleeping huts no longer properly secured? Can the food bowls tip over or are they damaged? If the answer is yes to any of these questions, you should immediately take care of that, so that the animals cannot injure themselves while jumping or playing.

Weekly Once a week there needs to be a major cleaning:

› Remove all hay from the cage and—if need be—clean the entire floor.

› Discard old dust in the dust/sand bath. Wash the dust/sand container thoroughly with hot water and let it dry. Refill with fresh dust.

Monthly Once a month, set time aside for a major cleaning and any necessary repairs.

› Even though you are removing fecal balls and soiled materials daily, some remnant materials stay behind, trampled solidly onto the sitting boards and onto the floor of the sleeping huts. This material needs to be scraped off with the aid a stiff brush.

› Urine soaked into the sitting boards or inside the huts not only smells bad, but it also leaves behind ugly spots. These can easily be removed with a stiff brush, using hot water with some lemon juice.

› Because chinchillas will chew on everything, you have to accept the fact that you have to repair and/or replace damaged items inside the cage frequently. Change all defective materials as well as the large climbing branches once a month. Carve new edges into the pumice-stone chews that have been rounded off by the constant chewing of these little rodents.

› In order for the animals to have sufficient diversity, you should install something new every month. For example, this can be a new set of stairs or a new climbing opportunity.

Making **vacation plans?**

What may be fun for us means stress for your chinchillas: Each change of residence and each car trip places a significant emotional burden on these sensitive rodents. Therefore, you must never take your chinchillas with you when you are going on vacation. Similarly, taking the animals to some caretaker for the period you are gone is not advisable.

WELL-PLANNED Start looking for a reliable vacation replacement early to take care of the animals in their accustomed home every day.

GETTING TO KNOW THE CARETAKER It would be ideal if the animals could become acquainted with the caretaker some time before you depart for your vacation. This gives them an opportunity to become somewhat familiar with this person.

INFORMATION THAT MUST BE PROVIDED Instruct the chinchillas sitter early in all essential daily and weekly maintenance tasks you expect her or him to perform. It is best to write down what type of food is used, and how much is to be given every day.

SUPPLIES Make sure that there is sufficient food of all varieties on hand. Similarly, the usual litter and possible replacement parts for the cage furnishings should be on hand.

FREE RUN The chinchillas can only enjoy the accustomed free run when they are familiar with the sitter. Only then will the animals return to their cage without stress.

FOR ANY EVENTUALITIES In a conspicuous location in your house, leave the telephone number and address of your veterinarian, and the number of your cell phone as well as your vacation address.

The Daily Health Check

Correct care and maintenance of your chinchillas is the best prevention against health problems.

An Important Indicator: Weight

The weight of the animals is a good indicator of their state of health. If it varies substantially or one of the animals loses a lot of weight, this is a warning signal. Therefore, you should get your chinchillas accustomed to the "weighing ritual."
› A kitchen scale is ideally suited for this purpose. The weight should be readable to the nearest .5 ounce (10 g).
› Lure each one onto the scale with a treat.
› Weigh your chinchillas every three days. Establish a written table for the weighing results, which will reveal any changes. Small variations are normal; however, when an animal loses 10 percent of its weight during a three-day period, consult a veterinarian immediately.

Things to Look Out For

Check your chinchillas closely every day, and you will quickly notice if there is something wrong with a particular animal.

Weakness and Pain Often unusual behavior is indicative of a disease:
› If you find an animal on the cage bottom with its ears folded back, it may be injured or it is too weak to climb onto a sitting board or into the sleeping hut.
› If a chinchilla in the dust/sand bath does not roll on its back, it may be too weak or in pain. If an animal rubs its nose or anal region conspicuously often in the sand, it may be itching or be in pain. In such cases, the chinchilla should be taken to a veterinarian.

Teeth All dental problems should be attended to by a veterinarian as quickly as possible.
› Healthy incisor teeth are orange colored. Lighter colored teeth suggest vitamin and mineral deficiencies.
› If a chinchilla keeps dropping food pellets, or crumbles pellets while chewing, the teeth may not be growing properly. A veterinarian should attend to the incorrect positions of premolars and/or molars.
› A wet chin is also evidence of an oral cavity or dental disease.

Respiratory passages Chinchillas breathe fast, which is visible along the flanks and on the nostrils.

This type of scale may be found in specialty food stores and on the Internet, and may come in very handy for obtaining exact weight.

1 TEETH The enamel of healthy incisor teeth is yellow orange. If brighter, something is not right with its nutrition or it has dental problems.

2 FIT FEET The soles of the hind feet have a leathery skin and rubber-like balls. They must be free of wounds, sores, and horny patches.

3 HEALTHY SKIN Injuries to the skin are most easily discovered by blowing into the fur. This is the only way injuries become visible.

› If a chinchilla opens its mouth in order to breathe, the animal is in severe respiratory distress. This requires immediate veterinary attention!

› Occasional sneezing after a dust/sand bath is normal; however, if an animal sneezes frequently, it may have contracted a cold. A veterinarian should attend to it.

› Nasal discharge is visible only when the animal has sustained a severe cold. Normally, chinchillas clean their snout with their front paws. Therefore, check the insides of the front paws. Encrustations, together with a discharge, are indicative of a cold.

Fur If the fur is matted, the chinchilla is not bathing enough in dust. If the fur around the eyes is matted, this may be indicative of an eye inflammation or dental problems.

Digestion Squashed fecal matter on the sitting boards or a dirty anal region suggests diarrhea.

Examination of fecal balls Normally, fecal balls are firm, smooth, and elongated to oval in shape. The size varies from one animal to the next. If fecal balls suddenly become smaller, this is indicative of constipation. If they are soft or you find fecal material smeared throughout the cage, the animals are suffering from diarrhea. Check for a change in diet and take the animal to the veterinarian.

Cecal feces Not to be mistaken for normal fecal balls, is fecal matter from the cecum. The animals will pick up these fecal balls directly from the anus and eat them. This is done to facilitate their digestion.

Estrus check of females If you are keeping males and females together, proper estrus control during the period of November through May is essential, in order to prevent breeding (see page 56).

Paws Check for excessive horny patches or actual injuries on the soles of the feet, which should be smooth and soft. Sores result from an incorrect diet and poor maintenance.

Ears Chinchilla ears are always slightly scaly, which is normal. If the ears are red or blood vessels are protruding noticeably, the chinchilla is too hot.

Injuries They are often difficult to spot in the dense fur of a chinchilla. If irregularities along the fur become conspicuous, blow gently to part the individual hairs so the skin becomes visible.

When a Chinchilla Is Sick

Chinchillas have a high metabolic rate. Therefore, diseases and poisonings progress very rapidly, so that the condition of affected animals can deteriorate quickly. Serious symptoms should be followed up immediately and so an urgent trip to the veterinarian is essential.

You must never treat chinchillas yourself, because the progress of a disease is often very complex, with symptoms similar to other conditions. Leave the diagnosis and therapy to your veterinarian. Even homeopathy and natural healing methods require knowledge and experience. Do not dispense home remedies on a mere suspicion.

Provide heat When chinchillas are sick, their body temperature drops. Normally, the body temperature is around 99°–101.3°F (37.2–38.5°C), and in juvenile animals it is 101.8–103.1°F (38.8–39.5°C). If a partic-

No appetite? For chinchillas, this is an alarm signal, and such an animal should be taken to a veterinarian immediately.

ular animal feels cool—especially around the ears—provide constant heat. The best way to do this is with a hot-water bottle. The animals can cuddle up to it as needed and avoid it when it is too hot. Infrared heat lamps are not suitable, because they are too hot and can cause burns.

When a Chinchilla Stops Feeding

When a chinchilla refuses food, the animal is in very serious danger. When the digestive track is completely empty, the intestinal flora dies off and the animal is being poisoned from the inside. When the body temperature drops below 101.4°F (38°C), circulation comes to a halt. Therefore, you must take the animal immediately to a veterinarian! A chinchilla that stops feeding must be force-fed from the first day on. This may sound terrible, but it is a lifesaving procedure for the animals. The veterinarian will show you how to feed the chinchilla, and he will provide you with suitable food. In an emergency, soften a few pellets in water and crush them into a mash, which is then administered with a syringe (with no needle).

> Insert the syringe laterally into the mouth behind the incisors, extend the head slightly and support it. Make sure that the chinchilla actually swallows and feeds slowly so that the food goes properly down the esophagus.

> A chinchilla with a weight of 17.6 ounces (500 g) requires 5 teaspoons (25 ml) of this mash per day, which should be administered in 3 to 5 portions at two-hour intervals.

> Feed your chinchilla only when it is awake. Waking up an animal causes additional stress.

Recognizing **Disease Symptoms**

SYMPTOM	CAUSE	WHAT TO DO?
Chinchilla feeds slowly, salivates, often touches its mouth or rubs it on the sitting board	Incorrect position of molars, tips of teeth are growing into cheek or tongue	Molars need to be filed back by veterinarian
Position and length of incisors deviate from normal condition	Not enough hay available	Provide lots of chewing materials, have teeth checked by veterinarian
Trampled feces sticks to sitting boards, encrusted anal region, animal slides anal region across sitting boards, and bathes more frequently	Diarrhea caused by change of diet, food incompatibility, or infection	Feed only hay and pellets; if there is no improvement next morning consult the veterinarian immediately
Chinchilla feeds poorly and fecal balls are getting smaller; the abdomen feels tight	Constipation due to change of diet or food incompatibility, hair balls, parasites	Diagnosis and therapy by veterinarian
Chinchilla feeds poorly and loses weight	Several causes could be involved	Immediate veterinary attention required
Chinchilla raises one paw, sits apathetically on the floor and hardly moves or appears clumsy	Injuries due to accident while jumping inside the cage or during free run	Diagnosis and therapy by veterinarian
Female: whitish discharge from vaginal opening outside estrus period, matted fur, increased sand bathing, and is aggressive	Inflammation of uterus	Diagnosis and therapy by veterinarian
Male: sits upright and looks frequently at anal region, penis is swollen and bluish	Penal prolapse due to hair ring	Moisten penis with chamomile tea, remove hair ring or take animal to a veterinarian
Loss of hair and changes of skin	Fighting with other chinchillas, injuries, parasites, fungi	Diagnosis and therapy by veterinarian
Chinchilla drinks a lot	Symptoms of various diseases	Diagnosis and therapy by veterinarian
Chinchilla breathes through mouth	Respiratory or cardiac problems	Take animal immediately to a veterinarian

Fun and Games

Chinchillas are highly intelligent. Communication and daily games with the others in the cage are essential for their emotional stability and physical health. Keeping them continuously in a cage is far too monotonous for them, so provide an extensive activity and fitness program.

Making the Search for Food Stimulating

In their natural habitat, chinchillas spend many hours every day in search of food, an activity not available to chinchillas kept in a cage. Therefore, provide their food not only in a bowl, but also deposited at various locations throughout the cage. Searching for food not only prevents boredom, but whoever discovers the tastiest treat must run a lot to secure the "prey" from the other family members. To do that, they hop around like kangaroos, with the food securely kept in their front paws.

> Distribute small pieces of food, such as herb stems or dried rose hips, throughout the cage, or hide them under a pile of hay.

> Offer occasionally a whole apple: Initially the chinchillas will roll it around; then they will enjoy eating such a treat. Remove it after they have taken a few bites so they don't eat too much of it and get diarrhea.

> Chinchillas look quite specifically for particular straws in the hay—and they spend quite a while sniffing and digging. You can further enhance the search for the perfect straw by offering so-called hay cobs. These consist of hay that has been compressed into large pellets. However, it is important that these do not contain honey or molasses.

> Chinchillas spend hours gnawing. Distribute pumice-stone chews of different sizes, as well as an ample amount of twigs and branches throughout the cage. Even untreated wooden blocks—either individually or threaded together—are eagerly gnawed on and chased after by the other chinchillas in the group. Parrot toys, made of natural wood, are favorites. They are safe for your chinchillas, but avoid toys that have stained wood.

This wasn't here yesterday! A new climbing branch provides diversity in the day of a chinchilla.

One, two, three in double quick time: anyone who busily works out on the exercise wheel not only trains his muscles, but also his sense of balance.

Tricky object: whole apples are a real challenge for chinchillas. How can one hold on to this thing? How can this delicious fruit be taken apart?

Always Keep Moving

Cage furnishings that include a fitness course made up of ramps and suspension bridges are at the heart of the chinchilla activity program. However, you must also offer diversity, by providing new climbing facilities regularly, a new suspension bridge in the cage, changing the position of climbing branches, or occasionally splurging for a new toy or exercise equipment.

> Untreated wooden blocks and balls make fascinating toys, as well as balls made out of willow twigs. They are fun to roll around in the cage and—of course—to take apart. Because chinchillas can become entangled with their legs in such balls, give them to the animals only under supervision.

> Pet shops also have special chinchilla running wheels. They are larger than traditional hamster wheels, which are unsuitable for chinchillas. Also very suitable are wooden wheels with a continuous running surface. Models with rungs or wire mesh are not suitable, because chinchillas can become entangled with their legs. Solid-surface wheels should be at least 18 inches (46 cm) in diameter, and have a 4–6-inch-wide running surface.

> "Flying saucer" exercise wheels are available that are ideal for chinchillas to work out on.

Important Attach the running wheel or disk securely inside the cage so that it cannot be knocked over by enthusiastic animals. Such equipment brings out the agility of chinchillas; not all animals like these particular toys, and many really have to practice until they are able to maintain their balance while "working out." Please be advised that some chinchillas become obsessed with running on a wheel or a saucer. If this is the case, your pet is probably bored and needs to have more interesting toys introduced, and its out-of-cage playtime increased.

To Top It All: A Climbing Tree

If there is sufficient room, set up a climbing tree that consists of a stem and many sitting boards at different levels. Place a few tasty treats on the boards, and your chinchillas will soon conquer this "playground" with great enthusiasm.

For Explorers and Adventurers: The Free Run

Irrespective of the size of your cage, chinchillas are curious and can hardly wait to explore outside their wire mesh enclosure. Therefore, the daily free run during the evening hours is essential for proper care and maintenance of these animals. Moreover, it is the high point of the chinchillas' day!

However, before the animals can embark on their discovery tour, they must be completely tame, because otherwise the excursion will involve a lot of stress for the animals. Kitchens, baths, or living rooms are not suited for this free-run adventure.

If possible, you should set up a dedicated "free-run room" for the animals. Ideally, this should be the room where the chinchilla cage is located. You must set up this room in such a way that it is free of potential dangers (see page 53).

› Chinchillas are agile climbers and can jump 3 feet (1 m) high and wide without a running start. Remove everything within reach of the animals that could be dangerous to them. Chinchillas can remember how far they have to jump, so you should not remove anything from the free-run

What happens next? After a brief rest at a vantage point, the chinchilla is ready to continue its exploration during the free run.

room after the initial excursion: If you do, these little acrobats can easily crash-land.

› Since chinchillas have an extraordinary sense of taste, they will chew on substances like cleaning agents, medicine tablets, and similar items. Remove all of this!

How the Free Run Becomes a Pleasure

Let the chinchillas out for their free run only when you have sufficient time—one hour is the absolute minimum. Allow time to supervise the animals without stress, where you you can attract the animals back into their cage at leisure.

› Provide a safe way for the animals to leave their cage. If it is elevated, install a safe stairway so the animals can climb safely out of the cage.

› Never leave the free-run room. Even in a safe room, something can be dislodged or tipped over by the jumping animals, which then could endanger their safety.

› Avoid any hectic, quick movements or loud noises. Chinchillas frighten easily and are then inclined to panic.

Variety is essential Even in the free-run room, there need to be appropriate changes to provide regular diversity:

› build a small labyrinth of earthenware and cork bark tubes, which can be easily rearranged to create a change.

› Place material such as wood, hay, or blank paper in an untreated willow basket and hide small treats to be discovered inside. It is fine if the basket is chewed on in the process.

› Chinchillas like to see what is happening around them. Set up small observation platforms with access stairways, or buy a climbing tree (see page 51).

› Gymnastic equipment, such as seesaws and other toys are much more interesting during the free run than back in the cage—keep offering the animals something new as often as possible.

› The free run is perfect only with a dust/sand bath. This must always be available to the animals.

Back into the cage Even the most fun-filled free run must eventually come to an end. Call them back to the cage with a calm voice and a tasty treat on the stairway to the cage or in the cage. Never chase the chinchillas—they will panic and you will lose their trust for a long time.

Avoiding Dangers During the Free Run

GNAWING The following materials do not belong in the free-run room: printed paper, treated wood (see page 40), leather, plastic, medicines, cosmetics, cleaning and washing materials, ornamental indoor plants, or electrical cables. Consult electrician!! Similarly, chinchillas like to chew on carpets. Therefore, uncovered floors are more suitable in the free-run room.

DANGERS OF ACCIDENTS Cupboards, drawers, doors, and pivot-hung windows can become traps for chinchillas. Install baby-proofing locks on cupboards and drawers. Make sure that the animals cannot become entrapped anywhere and injure themselves. Always keep doors and windows closed!

WATER Flower vases, watering cans, drinking glasses can easily be knocked over, frighten the animals, and get their sensitive fur wet.

Signs of Stress

Of course, chinchillas have different personalities: some are courageous daredevils; others are cautious "scaredy-cats." Yet, even though all of them have a "thick skin," in reality chinchillas are very sensitive creatures. They suffer greatly under stress. Fighting within the group, boredom, noise, and many other things can make them so sick that they die. Therefore, it is imperative that you constantly monitor the behavior of your chinchillas, so that you immediately notice anything unusual or conspicuous and then react promptly. Diseases, too, are often first recognizable by behavioral problems. Is the cage at the appropriate location? Are the animals

being disturbed during the day by loud voices, music, or television sets? If you are keeping two groups of chinchillas: Are the cages sufficiently far apart and is there an appropriate sight barrier between them? If any of these factors are not optimal, you should immediately correct them.

The Most Common Behavioral Disorders

Fur biting Hairless patches on chinchilla fur develop if an animal bites itself or is being bitten by members of the group. These patches are not completely bare but are covered by short dark hairs. Often there may only be apparent irregularities in the fur. If these bites are self-inflicted, the patches are commonly found above the origin of the tail, along the flanks, as well as on the lower arms. The reason can be boredom, fighting, the loss of a member of the group, or also pain and chronic diseases. If chinchillas bite the fur of one of the other group members, this manifests itself by the absence of fur tufts along the back, but also when the animals (as is possible among chinchillas) lose hair due to stress. This is due to problems within the group's hierarchy. If boredom is the reason, it is essential that you provide more diversity in the cage and during the free run. If changes in the hierarchy are the cause, the affected animal must be removed from the group. In that case you should try to start up a new group with this animal in another cage (see page 23).

Could there be something interesting inside? Healthy chinchillas are extremely curious. No corner in their cage is safe from their natural curiosity.

Cage rattling Sometimes chinchillas will rattle the cage wire with their front paws or they may chew on it in order to make a noise. If you react to that immediately, the animals will have learned how to attract your attention, or that they will then be allowed out on their free run. However, cage rattling is also often a sign of boredom. Make sure that there are new opportunities for different activities (see pages 50/51).

Urinating When chinchillas urinate in the dust/sand bath or in their food bowl, that could be a sign of problems within the hierarchy of the group—the animals have a greater tendency to "mark" their food. Change the food daily, and clean the dust/sand bath as well as the toilet corners.

Fighting within the chinchilla family Even in the best of families, there can be occasional arguments; however, when there is protracted fighting, it becomes essential for you to intervene. Even when a small group of animals is stable, there can be changes in the hierarchy, for instance, when one animal is getting old or becomes infirm, a group member dies, or offspring have grown up. Such "arguments" have become problematic when you notice that one chinchilla is always sleeping alone or gradually loses weight. If one group member is frequently chased through the cage or sits alone in a corner of the cage, it is high time for you to remove the animal from the group.

Spraying urine This defensive behavior is the highest alarm signal given off by a chinchilla (see page 18). Even if you are unable to see this taking place, you will be able to recognize animals sprayed with urine by the yellowish discoloration along the lower abdominal fur. If this behavior occurs frequently, you will need to find out the

Alarm Code Red! Rattling the cage wire is a serious behavior problem. The animals suffer from boredom. You must provide a quick remedy!

reason for this severe expression of fear and then proceed to eliminate the problem.

Vocalization If you hear too many alarm and panic calls (see pages 15/16), there is probably stress within the group. Monitor the animals closely and, if need be, split up the chinchilla group.

Stereotypes If one chinchilla continuously runs back and forth along one side of the cage or jumps from one sitting platform to another and back, it is a sign of extreme underactivity. Similar behavior can develop when there are insufficient hiding places. Eliminate the causes immediately.

Apathy If one chinchilla sits in a corner of the cage or on the bottom and does not react when it is talked to, you need to find out whether the animal is sick or is afraid of something. An apathetic chinchilla has given up on itself and needs help quickly! Take the affected animal out of the group and consult an experienced veterinarian.

Chinchilla Offspring

Can you handle the offspring? Do you have sufficient room or someone to take the youngsters?

Well Cared For: Chinchilla Babies

Depending upon the month of birth of chinchilla
females, their first estrus often occurs as early as
three to four months after they are born, but sometimes only after a full year. Chinchillas born in spring
will become sexually mature in the fall of the same
year. Animals born in fall do not reach sexual maturity
until the fall of the following year. Male chinchillas are
sexually mature at an age of four to six months.
> For a female to be able to handle a pregnancy
without complications, the animal should be one
to two years old, i.e., when it is fully grown.
> After a gestation period of about 111 days, one
to three young are born. Chinchillas do not build a
nest. Some will give birth on the cage floor, others
in the sleeping hut.
> Newborn chinchillas weigh barely 2.8 ounces
(80 g); however, they come into the world fully
developed and with their eyes open. After the birth,
the female cleans the young, which then also start
breathing. After a short period, the first contact
sounds can be heard, and the young may then even
start their first exploratory tours.
> After a few days, the youngsters hop around and
even sample the first stick of hay, yet their principal
food is mother's milk. Usually only two teats on the
mother will release milk, so make sure all babies
gain weight at the same pace.
> Under no circumstances should you remove the
other members of the group from the female and
her youngsters. Not only the father, but also all
other family members participate in raising the kits.
Only when several females are pregnant at the
same time can it come to physical arguments.
> At 12 weeks, the young are agile, feed them-
selves, and can be separated from the group.

Preventing Breeding

From November to May, chinchilla females are
ready to mate every four weeks. Estrus lasts for
three to five days; however, during that period the
male is accepted for mating only for 10 to 15 hours,
usually during the second night. From June to Octo-
ber chinchilla females cannot become pregnant.
> If you do not want to breed your animals, you will
need to make regular estrus checks on the females
during the period November through May. Caution:
females can become impregnated again immediately after the birth of a litter.
> During estrus, separate the male from the female
for three to five days. Insert a partitioning wall or
transfer him to another cage.

Ready to **Breed?**

MONITORING Below the vaginal cone is—
crosswise—the vaginal slot. It is normally closed,
but during estrus it opens up and a milky secre-
tion is discharged. For estrus control, you pick up
the chinchilla and check whether the slot is open.
If it is, keep the male separate.

CALENDAR Make a note of the days of estrus, so
that you need to check only during a few days
each month.

MINI VERSION Chinchilla babies are exact duplicates of their parents. At birth, they already have a dense fur and their eyes are open. It does not take long before the young give off soft squeaky sounds. This is their way of establishing contact with their mother. There is usually only one or two young per chinchilla female. The entire group participates in rearing the young: from father and aunts to the older siblings, the young learn the game rules within the chinchilla clan.

EARLY SKILLS Soon after their birth, young chinchillas follow the adults through the cage. Closely monitored by the mother and the group, they explore their new world. They appear to be just as curious as adult chinchillas. Everything they come across will be sniffed at and examined with a test bite.

COMPULSIVE NIBBLER Even though chinchilla babies feed only on mother's milk during the first few months, a cautious bite into a piece of apple or a few straws of hay is essential at that early age.

When Chinchillas Grow Old

With good care and maintenance, chinchillas can live to be quite old: In fact, they can reach an age of approximately 15 years, and even live longer than 20 years. However, old chinchillas have rather different requirements than young ones. Therefore, you have to adjust to these new demands from your chinchilla elders. Moreover, do not be alarmed when their appearance and behavior gradually change—that is quite normal.

› Do not be surprised when the fur becomes more and more patchy and loses its shiny appearance. Older animals are no longer capable of rolling around on their backs in the sand bath as actively as before; consequently, fur care becomes less effective.

› Old chinchillas become gradually thinner. Especially their neck and flanks start to cave in. The animals become increasingly selective with their food, and so you should avoid dietary changes—old chinchillas can hardly ever be converted to new types of food. Continue to supply ample amounts of fiber-

Everything as before—that is good news especially for old chinchillas. They prefer a more regulated day and somewhat more comfort, rather than wild adventures.

rich food, such as hay and pellets. You should be even more careful than before with treats; after all, older animals are substantially less active.

› Certain characteristics of your aging pets become more striking; there are many things they no longer tolerate. They stress out more readily. When disturbed, they vocalize more aggressively, and they insist on a strictly regulated daily routine.

› In many instances, their hearing and vision diminish. For that reason, older chinchillas frighten easily. In particular, avoid loud and unusual sounds.

› Old chinchillas no longer have the strength for long jumps and find it difficult to overcome steep inclines, so sitting boards should be interconnected with steps that are not too steep, and sleeping huts should be positioned lower in the cage. All these modifications should be done in small increments—chinchillas are creatures of habit and crash easily when things are no longer in their accustomed places or positions.

› In the end, often only a single chinchilla remains, because all the other members of the group have passed away. Usually there is little point in looking for a new partner for such an animal. A young chinchilla is far too active. It will quickly upset an older animal. Adding another, similarly lonely, senior partner rarely ever works out. Therefore, it is better to place more attention on your lone survivor.

A Heavy-Hearted Good-bye

No good-bye is easy. After 15 to 20 years, your chinchillas have become virtual family members. It is understandable that the loss of your pets is painful. If an animal is terminally ill, it is your responsibility not to let the animal suffer unnecessarily. As difficult as it is—you should have the animal put to sleep by a veterinarian.

Even though the silky fur of chinchilla veterans starts to show a few barren patches, their delightful mannerisms remain.

The Needs of Old Chinchillas

STEPS AND RAMPS Old chinchillas can no longer jump as well as young ones. Therefore, you should install low incline ramps leading up to their sleeping and viewing platforms. This will enable the animals to walk easily up to the higher levels in the cage.

REST Old chinchillas require a lot of rest. Therefore, a young, wild chinchilla as a replacement for a departed partner is usually not a good idea.

FIRM RULES Old chinchillas can handle stress even less than young ones. Therefore, establish firm, daily routines that suit the animals.

ATTENTION Even though old chinchillas are quieter, they need even more attention from you than before. Therefore, always have ample time for your pet seniors.

Clubs and Associations

> Empress Chinchilla Breeders Cooperative, Inc.
www.empresschinchilla.com

> Mutation Chinchilla Breeders Association
www.mutationchinchillas.com

> The Chinchilla Breeders Organization
www.chinchillabreeders.org/

> The Chinchilla Club
www.chinchillaclub.com

Chinchillas Online

First and foremost, you should direct specific questions about chinchillas to your local pet shop, the breeder who has provided your animals, and/or other chinchilla hobbyists in your vicinity. But a vast amount of information is also readily available on the Internet.

> *www.chinchillacorner.com*
> *www.echinchilla.com*
> *www.chincare.com*

Here is a wonderful link to chinchilla literature:

> *www.library-of-chinchilla-books.com*

Also available from Barron's

> *The Chinchilla Handbook* by Dr. Sharon Vanderlip, Barron's Educational Series, Inc., 2006.

Important Notes

> Sick chinchillas If there are disease symptoms in any of your chinchillas, these animals must be attended to immediately by a veterinarian.

> Risks of infection Only a few chinchilla diseases can be transmitted to humans. Advise your doctor or other attending medical professional about your animal contacts. This is particularly important in the event you have been bitten.

> Animal hair allergy Some humans can have allergic reactions to animal hairs or dander. If you are uncertain whether you have this condition, talk to your doctor before buying chinchillas.

The title of the German book is *Chinchillas*

English translation by U. Erich Friese

All inquiries should be addressed to:
Barron's Educational Series, Inc.
250 Wireless Boulevard
Hauppauge, NY 11788
www.barronseduc.com

ISBN-13: 978-0-7641-4293-2
ISBN-10: 0 7641 4293-3

Library of Congress Control No.: 2009010416

Library of Congress Cataloging-in-Publication Data
Bartl, Juliana.
    [Chinchillas. English]
    Chinchillas / author, Juliana Bartl; photographer,
Ulrike Schanz.
        p. cm.
        Includes index.
        ISBN-13: 978-0-7641-4293-2
        ISBN-10: 0-7641-4293 3
    1. Chinchillas as pets. I. Title.

    SF459.C4813B37 2010
    636.935'93—dc22   2009010416

PRINTED IN CHINA
9 8 7 6 5 4 3 2 1

The Author

Dr. Juliana Bartl is a veterinarian who has
been working with chinchillas for 16 years.
She was awarded her doctorate degree at
the Institute for Behavioral Sciences and
Animal Welfare (*Institut für Verhaltenskunde
und Tierschutz*), Ludwig-Maximilan-University in Munich, for her dissertation "The
Vocalization of Chinchillas within a Social
Group" (*Die Lautäußerungen der Chinchillas
im Sozialverband*). Since 2006, she has
been working in her own veterinary practice,
with special emphasis on rabbits, rodents,
and chinchillas.

The Photographer

Ulrike Schanz has been working for
15 years as a freelance photographic
designer, with emphasis on pet photography. Her photographs appear in many
national and international magazines and
advertising brochures. Further details
about her photo studio are available from
www.schanz-fotodesign.de.

Photo References

All photographs in this book by Ulrike
Schanz, with the exception of: Alamy/Art
Wolfe: page 6; NHPA/Kitchin & Hurst:
page 7.

SOS – What to Do?

Fighting in the Chinchilla Home

PROBLEM A chinchilla is being chased by another one, or it has sustained a bite injury or it sits by itself on the bottom of the cage. **SOLUTION** Take the animal out of the group and place it in a separate cage. You may be able to use the animal as the nucleus for starting up a new group.

Hair Loss

PROBLEM There are tufts of hair scattered throughout the cage. The chinchillas are either biting each other or one animal keeps pulling out its own hair. **SOLUTION** Biting hairs is a sign of stress within the group or incorrect maintenance conditions. Find out the cause and eliminate it as quickly as possible.

A Chinchilla Stops Eating!

PROBLEM If a chinchilla stops eating, that is an emergency on the very first day. **SOLUTION** Take the animal immediately to a veterinarian in order to find out the reason. He will also show you how to feed the animal with a special mash until it recommences eating on its own. Check the weight daily!

Escaped!

PROBLEM One or more chinchillas have managed to get out of the cage and are on the loose in your home. **SOLUTION** Move cautiously when looking for the animals and make sure that you do not squash the animals inadvertently behind doors or in drawers. Once you have discovered the escapees, approach them with a calm voice and try to attract them to your hand. Then cautiously pick them up. Better yet; shake the bag with treats noisily and lay out a tempting track of treats in the direction of the cage door. Very important: never chase chinchillas. These animals panic easily and will then undertake high-risk escape maneuvers.

Apathy

PROBLEM A chinchilla sits on the cage bottom and is too weak to climb up into the sleeping hut. **SOLUTION** Check whether the animal has been eating or whether it has been injured. Take it to a veterinarian as soon as possible. Only he or she can determine the cause of such apathetic behavior during a thorough examination.